D1142143

Just
the Right
WORDS

Just
the Right
WORDS

JUDITH WIBBERLEY

D&C

David and Charles

In loving memory of my father
James Frederick Burgess (1921–1964)

A DAVID & CHARLES BOOK
Copyright © David & Charles Limited 2007

David & Charles is an F+W Publications Inc.
company
4700 East Galbraith Road
Cincinnati, OH 45236

First published in the UK in 2007

Text copyright © Judith A. Wibberley 2007
Illustrations copyright ©
David & Charles 2007

Judith Wibberley has asserted her right to be
identified as author of this work in accordance with
the Copyright, Designs and Patents Act, 1988.

All rights reserved. No part of this publication
may be reproduced, stored in a retrieval system,
or transmitted, in any form or by any means,
electronic or mechanical, by photocopying,
recording or otherwise, without prior permission
in writing from the publisher.

A catalogue record for this book is available
from the British Library.

ISBN-13: 978-0-7153-2637-4 hardback
ISBN-10: 0-7153-2637-6 hardback

ISBN-13: 978-0-7153-2636-7 paperback
ISBN-10: 0-7153-2636-8 paperback

Printed in Singapore by KHL Printing Co Pte Ltd
for David & Charles
Brunel House   Newton Abbot   Devon

Commissioning Editor Jane Trollope
Desk Editor Bethany Dymond
Art Editor Sarah Underhill
Designer and Illustrator Emma Sandquest
Project Editor Natasha Reed
Production Controller Ros Napper

Visit our website at www.davidandcharles.co.uk

David & Charles books are available from
all good bookshops; alternatively you can
contact our Orderline on 0870 9908222 or
write to us at FREEPOST EX2 110, D&C
Direct, Newton Abbot, TQ12 4ZZ (no
stamp required UK only);
US customers call 800-289-0963 and Canadian
customers call 800-840-5220.

Contents

Acknowledgments

With special thanks to my husband Colin, my knight in shining armour, who always knew that I would be published one day, with inspiration, support and love also provided by my daughter Deborah who was my proof-reader, her partner Adrian, my son James, my daughter-in-law Angela, my lovely grandson Luke James and my family for whom many of these verses were written. These verses owe much to those who I have loved and lost at an early age but moreover to those who have been exceptional friends throughout my life such as Ethel Houghton, Deborah Forrest, Su Marshall, Barbara and Keith Milton and so many more who know who they are. Friendship is such a precious gift from God and He has certainly bestowed on me some of the most treasured moments and memories from true angels here on earth, my thanks to God and all of them from the bottom of my heart, these words are for you.

Every good and perfect gift is from above, *James 1:17*

Introduction

A beautiful collection of original card makers' verses and illustrations with poignant words for every occasion, written especially for handmade card makers and for those who wish to add an extra special personal touch to an otherwise blank card. Amongst the everyday greetings and salutations specially written for this book you will find extra special verses written straight from the heart. Words that were inspired by treasured moments spent with special friends and dearest relatives, some present, some past, who brought colour, comfort and love into the author's life. These heartfelt and touching card verses capture and express many moments, thoughts, feelings and emotions not found in conventionally produced greeting cards for the mass market. They will bring life to any specially created handmade card, they will add the final touch of elegance and expression to your work of art but above all these original verses will bring joy to your heart, a smile to your face and will prove an invaluable point of reference for your card crafting and greeting needs. Simply go to the appropriate section, whether it be birthdays or bereavement, and find the verse you most identify with.

Anniversaries

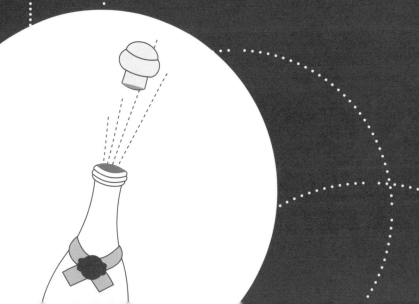

On Our Special Anniversary

I may not always show you
And I may not always say
How much you really mean to me
In every kind of way

So on this special day of ours
I would like the world to know
How much I really need you
And how I truly love you so

tip

You can easily adapt this verse for any type of anniversary by changing the word 'golden' and substituting the number of years

On Your Golden Wedding Anniversary

Fifty glorious years together
Memories recent, many old
May all of them be treasured
For they have turned to gold

On Our Wedding Anniversary

I wouldn't change a single day
That I have spent with you
There's love in everything you say
In everything you do
You never need to tell me
How much you love me so
For every time I look at you
Your smile just lets me know

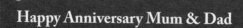

Happy Anniversary Mum & Dad

*The love you have for each other
is an inspiration to all of us
a firm rock which helped me
to be the person I am today
proud to call you, Mum and Dad*

Celebrate the love you have for each other
Recapture happy memories long forgotten
Cherish your life together always
On this, your anniversary

On your Silver Wedding Anniversary

It seems like only yesterday
That you both said 'I do'
The years have gone so quickly
And been so kind to you
Lots of memories to hold on to
Love and laughter on the way
Treasure them and one another
On your Silver Wedding Day

*May this Wedding Anniversary Day
bring together a collection
of beautiful memories
and create dreams of
more precious tomorrows*

*Each passing year brings me
closer to you
so close that I can feel
what you feel
love what you love
and know that you were
truly heaven sent*

HAPPY ANNIVERSARY DARLING

Just to say........

of all the people in
all the world I'm
glad I married you
Happy Anniversary
Darling

*You're always there
each time for me*
When everything goes wrong
You cheer me up and make me laugh
You keep our marriage strong

You're my best friend, my husband
My lover and much more
The man I love so very much
The man that I adore

I'm so glad that you asked me
Years ago to be your wife
The one to share your hopes and fears
The one to share your life

And at this special time of year
There's nothing more to say
Than to wish you all you wish yourself
On our Anniversary

No child could wish for parents
More loving than you two
A daughter could not hope for
More support to see her through
You laid a firm foundation
On which to build my life
So I could be a mother
A best friend and a wife
Thank you for being rock solid
Through the good times and the bad
But most of all I bless you both
For being my Mum and Dad

HAPPY ANNIVERSARY

Husband/Wife

I love you so, you're always there
To comfort me and show you care
I know you always understand
I feel upset, you touch my hand
You are my reason to exist
I knew that moment we first kissed
I cherish our anniversary
The day on which you married me
You are the person I adore
So here's to many, many more

Happy Anniversary Darling

Marriage is a priceless gift
That makes two people one
That binds them with a love so strong
To help them carry on

Through ups and downs life hands them
Happy days and sometimes sad
That helps them to discover
What it's like as Mum and Dad

To build a world together
A precious family of their own
To find a house together
That then becomes a home

Marriage is a treasure
That can't be bought or sold
It's a partnership together
Which, with the years, can turn to gold

HAPPY GOLDEN WEDDING

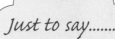

Just to say........

you made two half
families into a
great whole one
Happy Anniversary
to you both from all
of your children

*Life is not always easy
but being with you
and sharing our lives
is a pleasure that I hope
will last forever*

*You really are an angel
With everyone you meet
You're the wife I always dreamed of
You make my life complete*

HAPPY ANNIVERSARY

HAPPY ANNIVERSARY HUSBAND

*Reflections in the water on a lovely sunny day
Remind me of the day we met and I'd just like to say
You fill my life with sunshine like a thousand sparkling beams
You're my knight in shining armour, the answer to my dreams
The day we wed seems distant, so far away and yet
It was magical, a fairytale, a day I won't forget
For me it was so special, the beginning of my life
I'm proud of you my husband, proud to be your wife*

tip

Insert the number of years
that the couple have been
married in the first line,
to make it specific to
the anniversary

Son & Daughter-in-law
Or Daughter & Son-in-law

Three years you've spent together
As devoted man and wife
And now somebody special
Is about to share your life
You're a really lovely couple
Who both of us adore
About to make us 'grand' parents
Well who could ask for more
So on your anniversary
We wish you both good cheer
For your wedding celebrations
And throughout the coming year

Valentine's Day

I love you for being you
Where you are is where
I always want to be
My forever love

tip

For a special Valentine's
message for your wife,
simply substitute the word
'life' in line 6 with 'wife'

The magic of the love we share
Begins and ends with you
A love like this, they say, is rare
And that is very true
You're my best friend,
My love, my life
Without you, I'm incomplete
I look at you, I hold your hand
My heart still skips a beat
I can't believe I've found you
I count my blessings you are mine
My soulmate to the end of time
My Special Valentine

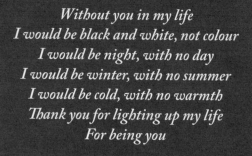

Without you in my life
I would be black and white, not colour
I would be night, with no day
I would be winter, with no summer
I would be cold, with no warmth
Thank you for lighting up my life
For being you

I may not always tell you
What I'm feeling deep inside
The emotions and the feelings
That I sometimes tend to hide
But I'm really proud and pleased
To know that you are mine
And I hope that you still love me
My Darling Valentine

*L*ove makes the world
go round they say
And that is very true
For when we met on that first day
I fell in love with you
I felt a kind of tingle, I do believe it's love
Like being shot with arrows
From Cupid up above
I never want to lose this wild and dreamy glow
These feelings of great passion
So I thought I'd let you know
That if you feel quite dizzy and fuzzy in the head
You're not falling for some illness,
You're just 'in love' instead
I hope you feel just like this,
That you're not feeling fine
My one true love, my hero
My darling Valentine

There is a special place in my heart for you
Remember that always
And know that no matter what
I am always there

tip

This verse (right) would be
ideal to accompany a
bouquet of flowers on
Valentine's Day

You're a very special person
Much too special to forget
So I thought I'd send my love to you
As I haven't done that yet

I want to tell you just how magical
You have made my life
And how some day, I hope that you
Will consent to be my wife

You look at me and all I know
Is that I will always love you so
You have truly captured my heart
But then I knew that from the start
I hear your voice, it calls my name
And in my dreams I do the same
I really wish you could be mine
My secret, special Valentine

I care for you and you know why
For I'll love you 'till the day I die
You hurt – and I feel the pain
And when you're sad – I feel the same

You need to talk – I'm there for you
A faithful friend, who's always true
We live our lives, not always together
But the love we share will last forever

Three words are not enough
To tell you just how I feel
My love for you is endless
All consuming and so real

You're in my head on waking
And all the whole day through
Inside my heart is breaking
Because it holds my love for you

Just to say........

you bring
sunshine
into my life

*L*ife goes by us so quickly

Sometimes there isn't time to say
How much I really love you
Each and every day

I love you for the little things
You say and do for me
For taking care of our lovely home
And our beautiful family

You are my soulmate, my love
And my best friend
Without you walking by my side
My happiness would end

So on this day for lovers
I'm sending all my love
For you truly are my angel
Sent from God above

tip

This would make an ideal
verse for a bookmark as
a keepsake

Love &
Friendship

*Nothing is more precious in life
than our closest friends
the ones we can depend on, trust
and confide in no matter what
the ones who have seen us through
the worst of times as well as the best of times
they are the rarest of all treasures,
angels in disguise*

*M*ay the love,
laughter and joy
you bring into other peoples' lives
be returned to you ten-fold
on this special day
and in the years to come

I hope today's the kind of day
That makes you smile out loud
That brings out rays of sunshine
From behind a lonely cloud
The kind of day that's special
For that's what I wish you
My dearest friend, who's always there
And is forever true

As the time passes by
and the sun sets on another day
so the seasons change
and the world takes on new meaning
but one thing remains unchanged
our friendship

Just to say........

you are the rarest of all flowers
that bloom in God's garden
you are the kindest of God's angels
that He sent to befriend us
you will forever be in my heart
that rejoices for knowing you
my world is a happier place
knowing that you walk beside me
my forever love

Days we've shared together
Memories from the past
Thoughts and dreams
We talked about
These are things that last

That's how it is with Friendship
Two minds that think as one
Laughing at such silly things
Long after they have gone

Friends don't need special occasions
Or anniversaries to say
Just how much a friendship means
Regardless of the day

*Love makes
all things possible
and dreams
come true*

*A close friend
is a precious gift from God
an angel in disguise*

*Life without friendship
has no meaning,
for it is like the sky
without the sun*

*My life is richer
for knowing you
you are a treasure
beyond compare*

*F*riends are
like orchids
created with love
bringing colour and harmony
into your life
rare and beautiful

*If I had to choose
between you and chocolates
I would pick you*

*A cheery note
From an old friend
Brings loving thoughts
Makes sadness end*

tip

The second verse can stand
alone as a gift tag or a
quick card if the word
'but' is omitted

I may not always tell you
How much your friendship means to me
There may not be many letters
Nor words for you to see

But on days when I feel lonely
And sometimes when I'm blue
A smile lights up my face
Because I know there's always you

To remind me that no matter
What begins or how it ends
You will always be there for me
We will always be good friends

So I always hold on to that truth
That warming heartfelt thought
That friends like you are treasures
Life without you would be naught

I love the way
you have of turning
special moments
into wonderful days

Just to say........

I don't need a special
occasion to say
'I love you'

You are the ear that listens
A light that guides the way
The smile that makes things better
That chases fears away
And when the burden's heavy
You lighten up the load
With gestures kind and simple
You're a friend worth more than gold

33

O
My Friend
often, I think of you
remember things you said
smile at memories so precious
reflect on all the silly moments
that make ours a great friendship
one that has stood the test of time
and remained so strong even though
distance keeps us from meeting too often
and I know God meant us to feel a special bond

LOVE

*

True friends don't need to
always keep in touch
when they have a
special bond
between
them

May the Sun
warm your heart with love
and the Moon
light your life with wonder
so that the Stars
can make your dreams come true

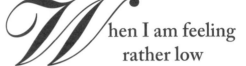

*There are good friends
and there are old friends
you are a good old friend
and a rare treasure*

hen I am feeling
rather low
And wondering what to do
I count my blessings for I have
A kind, wise friend like you

*Smile, though you feel like crying
Laugh, even though you're sad
Be glad that the rain is falling
And life won't feel half so bad
Try to look on the bright side
Even though the outlook is dim
Ask for God's help, He is near you
At times when you need Him*

Special Birthdays

1st Birthday

May the day be filled with laughter
And the parcels full of fun
The cards be packed with magic
For a birthday (girl) boy who's one

HAPPY 1st BIRTHDAY

2nd Birthday

Lots of birthday wishes
Are sent to you today
Some cuddles and some kisses
Are also on the way
Lots of presents and some cake
Are waiting just for you
To celebrate this happy time
The day that you are two

Birthday
Wishes

4th Birthday

You fill a room with magic
No Mum and Dad could ask for more
Our love and special wishes
On this day that you are four

3rd Birthday

Birthday wishes come your way
For a busy little bee
Who's opening his presents
Because today he's three

You can adapt this verse for
a girl by changing any
references to 'he' to 'she'

5th Birthday

You're five years old today
And growing up so fast
Hope this day of yours
Is full of fun and games
And memories that last

6th Birthday

*A little birdie told me
That you are six today
So this card is full of wishes for
A jolly good birthday*

7th Birthday

*The angels are all singing
Like a chorus up in heaven
For a darling little girl
Who is good and lucky seven*

8th Birthday

Get out the streamers, blow up the balloons
It's time to celebrate
For birthday time is here again
And this time round you're eight

HAVE A WONDERFUL TIME

tip

The above verse can also
be altered for use on 28th,
38th, 48th birthdays,
and so on

18th Birthday

May your wishes and dreams
become reality
now that you have come of age

18th Bithday

Today is full of laughter
Childhood dreams from yesterday
Hopes and ambitions for tomorrow
Now don't seem so far away
Life is there within your reach
Take and hold it, if you can
On this day that you'll remember
The day that you became a man

21 *st* Birthday

May the stars up in the heavens
Shine down to light your way
When you celebrate your birthday
On your very special day
Party on until it's sunrise
Till all the stars have gone
There will never be another day
When you are 21

CONGRATULATIONS

When we are young we count the months
when we are youths we add the years
when we are middle aged we drop the years
when we reach old age we are proud of our years
eventually we forget the years
and just have fun when it's our birthday

HAVE FUN ON YOUR BIRTHDAY
Whatever age you are

30th

It's no use getting in a strop
Or even getting shirty
Today's the day you face up
To really being thirty

Just to say........

it's not how old we look,
it's how old we feel
that matters.
Enjoy your day,
enjoy life

40th

They say, being forty, you're over the hill
But try being naughty and give life a thrill
Do all of those things that you wanted to do
Go out and enjoy yourself, find the real you
Tap into those feelings that you try to hide
And discover the child that is hiding inside
For life can be hectic and pass by us so soon
So reach for the stars and head for the moon

50 today

*You just don't look that old
All of your years now
Have turned into gold*

*Sixty glorious years of memories,
and many more to look forward to*

tip

*This verse (left) can be used
for any age over 50 as
the number is at the
beginning of the line*

Time has give you a beauty
In laughter lines upon your face
To show the world your kindness
Good humour and your grace

Happy 70th birthday

Each day more precious than the last,
you mean the world to me
You smile as you rest your eyes,
gathering roses in the gardens of memory

May your 90th birthday be as special as you

New Home

Home
Sweet
Home

GOOD LUCK IN YOUR NEW HOME

*May your new home bring you
good friends to your door
and fill your rooms with love
laughter and happiness*

*May this be the beginning
of something so wonderful
that you will treasure it
all of your life
hope you find a world of excitement
and a wealth of love*

Wishing you sunshine
to fill your rooms with joy
a garden full of life's treasures
and years of love and contentment
in your new home

You bring such joy to those around you
So wherever you may roam
You add a sparkle and some magic
That makes a house a home

GOOD LUCK WITH THE MOVE

A house is
made of
Walls and beams
But a home is filled
With love and dreams

Home
Sweet
Home

tip

The word 'house' can be
replaced by flat, apartment,
digs or home, depending on
the situation

*As you move into your new house
may you find love, laughter
and good fortune
knocking at your door*

A cottage in the country
A villa out in Spain
A little flat in London
Apartments on the Seine
Location does not matter
As long as where you roam
Love is always with you
Makes your house into a home

Sorry to tell you
That we've moved away
But here's our address
Should you want to come stay

....

....

Clothes are strewn, books aren't stacked
My treasured things are still unpacked
But even though it's such a mess
We love it at our new address

Just to say........

thank you for your
new home gift,
it was just what
we needed

We've finally settled
The moving was rough
We never imagined
We had so much stuff
The house is now tidy
The garden is too
The only thing missing
A visit from you

Weddings & Commitment

May you cherish these moments
For all of your life
As you step out together
As man and as wife
May the vows that you've taken
Remain true and strong
As you start on life's highway
And journey along

Three wishes on this special day
Of love, good health and laughter
Are sent to you so we can say
Live happily ever after

May you always be as close
And as happy as today
Support each other through your lives
And laugh along the way
May you always see the bright side
Even though it may go dim
May he love you and protect you
And may you do the same for him

Our sincere and heartfelt wishes
go out to you both
on the announcement of this happy occasion
congratulations for your forthcoming marriage
we would be pleased to attend

*May God bless you both
as you stand before Him
exchanging vows to each other
and speaking words of love
may He walk with you always*

*These heartfelt congratulations are sent
to a couple who were truly meant to be together
may the joy you bring to others
be returned to you on this happy day*

I
wish
you both
all you desire for
anyone who knows you
knows this love was meant to be
you're just a perfect match together
and this love you have is plain to see
so as you both join your hands together
exchange special words and rings of love
may heaven smile down to bless you both
and many glad tidings reign down from above

Congratulations on your commitment to each other

XXX
X

*You have made a promise within your hearts
to each other that will take a lifetime to fulfil*

Congratulations on your engagement

As you begin your lives together
Remember all the ways
You told each other how you felt
In those early days

Capture all those moments
And hold them in your soul
As you join yourselves together
To make a perfect whole

When hard times come upon you
Take those memories out once more
Stand together both united
And show trouble out the door

Know that each supports the other
In the good times and the bad
Take time to love one another
And don't make each other sad

Be a friend, soul-mate and lover
Let there be no yours and mine
Blend your hearts and minds together
Then your love will stand the test of time

Congratulations on your engagement
for you are starting on a journey
that will lead to great love

Marriage and Commitment
Is a strong and powerful tie
Binds two hearts together
As the years go passing by

Cherish every moment of this wonderful day
shine as you have never shone before
the centre stage is yours alone today
may you both live and love the moment
and treasure it in your memories always

Your lovely invitation was such a surprise
You finally decided to tie the knot
I could not believe my eyes
I'm busy now with what to wear
I'm over the moon, of course I'll be there

An engagement is a promise
of your forthcoming marriage
creating your own home together
filled with hopes, memories and dreams

I'm so very glad you're the man in my life
I'll make you so pleased you chose me your wife
On this special occasion, on our wedding day
As I walk on towards you, one thing I will pray
That these feelings we have will grow stronger with time
That I'll always be yours and you'll always be mine

On this day of our devotion
To one another before friends
Let us capture the emotion
Hope our true love never ends

May this beginning
of your lives together
never have an end

Before this special day is over
And each and everyone departs
Both step back and share the moments
Keep them forever in your hearts
For all too soon this day is over
So take the time to hold it near
It is a time of celebration
A time of loving and good cheer

Congratulations on your Wedding Day

As we stand up there together
Both as equals making one
As we make this, our commitment
May the memories linger on
For our love will grow each day
That we share with one another
You are my life, I'm glad to say
My best friend and my lover

As you join your hands this day
exchanging words and rings of love
may the heavens truly bless you both

Cherish every moment
of this wonderful day
Shine as you have never shone before
The centre stage is yours alone today
May you both live and love the moment
And treasure it in your memories always

61

Exams &
Graduation

Congratulations on a fantastic result
we always knew you would pass
but what an honour you did so well

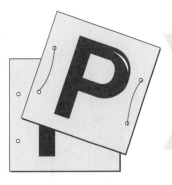

Results are in, here's to the date
When you will go and graduate
Congratulations

Glad that all the hard work
finally paid off
with such a great pass mark
you must be so pleased
Congratulations

Tear up the L plates

Throw them away
You passed the test
What a great day

*Congratulations
to the new driver
may this be the beginning
of a great adventure for you
now you have passed your test
may God watch over and protect you
as you travel far on the highway of life*

Three long years it took you
And some of them you hated
But we knew it would be worth it
On the day you graduated

There were days you didn't want to go
When you'd rather stay in bed
And the morning after revision nights
When you felt that you were dead

But everything was worth the climb
To reach up for that star
You've got the paper in your hand
That will take you near and far

We are proud you made the effort
Put in all that work and strife
May heaven reward you richly now
And forever throughout your life

Congratulations on Graduating

Just to say........

we are proud of you
And your great results
And all the hard work
You put in to get them

Well done on making all the grades
We knew that you had passed
Sleepless nights were worth it
You're a GRADUATE at last

On your Graduation Day

Sending you a day full of sunshine
A heaven filled with rainbows
And a pocket full of dreams
May the future ahead of you
Be as wonderful as you are

Just to say........

you made the grade,
you will go far,
so here's the keys
to your new car

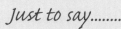

*So pleased that all your hard work
Has been recognised and rewarded
So that the world is now your oyster
From which you will reap great rewards*

*Congratulations are in order
For someone who's passed the test
We all knew that you could do it
As you always do your best*

WELL DONE

You're straight As in my book
Good Luck with the exams
Hope all your hard work pays off

Results are in and here's to fame
As you put those letters
After your name

CONGRATULATIONS

*We always knew you could beat the odds
And get the results you deserve*

WELL DONE

*M*ay these results
give you
A firm foundation
On which to build
A great future
In Life

Just to say........

you now have the paper
firmly in your hold
make your dreams
reality and your
future will unfold

Everyone loves a winner
And with those results
The sky is the limit

WELL DONE

Across the Miles

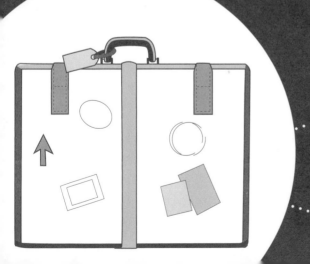

There's not much to tell you,
nothing to say
Except that I love you
more every day
Although we are parted
by so many miles
We capture in letters
our sorrows and smiles
We share something special,
a love that won't end
A closeness of spirits
known only to friends

Whilst I'm away…remember that I love you
say goodnight at our special hour
and know you are always in my heart

Sending lots of heartfelt wishes
So far across the sea
With millions of kisses
To you with love from me
You're a brother who is special
In every kind of way
So celebrate your life in full
On your 50th Birthday

tip

Make the above verse
suitable for any age and
relative by substituting
'50th' for any number and
'brother' for your relation

Though the miles may keep us apart

You will always be there in my heart
Missing you more than words can say
And waiting for that special day
When we are together once more

You are never far though miles away
From our loving thoughts each single day
Remembered in smiles and things we do
Parted by miles but close at heart are you

Just to say........
of all the friends who
have passed by you will
always be 'special',
may good fortune
follow you always as
you journey on in life

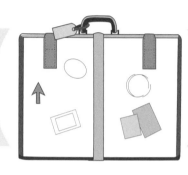

May God love and protect you
Whilst you are far away
And angels walk there with you
To make it safe along the way
For you are such a special person
Who means the world to me
My love grows stronger with each day
You are away across the sea
With every passing week
And each and every tide
I'm counting all the hours
Till you're home here by my side

I miss you so I must confess
Whilst you are far away
So hurry home to me again
I'm counting every day

*As you travel the world to experience life
and to look at what man has achieved in the world
take time to marvel at the beauty and wonderment
of nature that God created for us all to enjoy*

*Sending you love and joy, on this your special day
And missing you more than mere words could ever say
For though the miles may keep us all apart
You and your family are always closest to my heart
I pray each day for God to keep harm from your door
And count the days until I see you all once more*

tip

An alternative fourth line
to the verse below could be
- May St Christopher
protect you

Standing on a sandy shore looking out to sea
Each wave that breaks beneath my feet
Brings back your memory
May God protect you on your travels
And bring you safe back home to me

Wherever you walk in life
God is always by your side

*D*well not upon the
sadness of yesterday
but rather look forward
to the promise of a new tomorrow
seek out new adventures
gather new acquaintances around you
and feel God's love

Just to say........

*I hope your journey
leads you to happiness
and contentment*

Birthdays

*Hoping your birthday is filled
with joy and laughter
and all the wonderful things
a person like you deserves*

*Another year gone by so fast
Your birthday's here again
Take time to make the magic last
Make the memories remain
Capture all the moments
Hold them to you near
As time keeps moving forward
To another one next year*

You can't touch happiness
but you can feel it
wrapping its warm arms
around you
hope today is your happiest ever
you deserve the best of everything
all that life has to offer

Sending you birthday kisses
wrapped up in special wishes
for you to have the kind of day
that someone as lovely as you deserves

Hugs and kisses
Lots of birthday wishes
Especially for

YOU

*Wishing you all the good things in life,
happiness, friendship and chocolates*

tip

Switch this verse for
women by changing the
word 'husband' to 'wife'

*I hope today's the kind of day
To make you smile out loud
That brings out rays of sunshine
From behind a lonely cloud
The kind of day that's special
Is what I wish for you
My dearest darling husband
With all my love and kisses too*

81

The days go by so quickly
I just can't believe it's true
That it's been over one whole year
Since I sent a card to you
I'm really very sorry
That this year it is late
But late or not I hope that you
Went out to celebrate

Hope it was a good one
Happy Belated Birthday

I tell you how I love you
Almost every single day
So now on your birthday
There is little left to say
Than to wish you
All your dreams come true
And to hope that I
Share all of them with you

*L*ooked up,
        saw the date
Thought of you, my bestest mate
Ran with your card to the man
Who put it in a mail van
So it's in his hands, if by fate
Your birthday card should turn up late

Hope you have a Wizard Time
One from a magic spell
You're a very special person
So hope your day goes well

You don't look any older
so I had no prior warning
that another birthday
was on the horizon

Birthday Wishes for a Dear Friend

Friends don't need special occasions
or anniversaries to say
just how much a friendship means
regardless of the day

My dearest and treasured friend
may this day bring laughter into your life
happiness into your home
and joy to your heart
as you celebrate the day God sent us an Angel

For a Special Daughter's Birthday

The day you were born
God blessed us with love
As he touched all our lives
From heaven above

He gave us someone so special,
Unique and so rare
An Angel from Heaven
For whom we could care

You're our most precious treasure
A child we adore
We are two lucky parents
Who could not ask for more

Happy Birthday Darling,
may it be as special as you are

This envelope is not large enough
To carry all my love and wishes
Nor is there space enough to tell you
How much I treasure all your kisses

Imagine a love so boundless
That it is greater than the sea
Then you might get an idea
Just how much you mean to me

May your day be filled with rainbows
For you deserve them, every one
And may loving thoughts surround you
Long after the day is done

Happy Birthday, my love

tip

You can easily adapt this
verse for a special birthday,
just insert a number at the
end. For example, 'Happy
50th Birthday, my love'

For a Darling Grand Daughter

You arrived in my heart and held on tight
A shining star, so pretty and bright
An Angel of Love sent from God afar
May you always be loved and as sweet as you are

Happy Birthday, Son

You're Mummy's little soldier
You're Daddy's great big boy
You're Grandma's little helper
To us you're such a joy
So on this very special day
We send our love to you
For a day of fun and laughter
And lots of presents too

Jump up and down
Shout hip-hooray
Because you are so special
And so is your birthday

New Baby

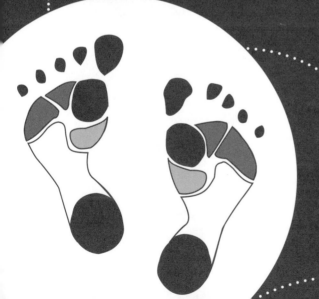

*A grand child is all of the joy
without the hard work
Congratulations*

On the Birth of Your Son

*May this special time be filled with joy
To welcome here your little boy
And time with him bring only pleasure
With memories you'll always treasure*

Congratulations to the proud Grand Parents

A grandchild is a joy doubled
is happy days revisited
and memories rekindled
it is God blessing you again
with the miracle of life

A daughter is so special
She will fill your life with love
Like a rainbow made with sunshine
When rain falls from above
Precious memories she will give you
Many heartaches and some tears
She's a treasure that is priceless
That will last you all your years

A bouquet of love
especially for you
on the birth of our first child

A family is a
little world
created with love and
nurtured by commitment

Congratulations on your new arrival

Congratulations on the Birth of your Baby

Days filled with laughter
A joy to behold
A treasure from Heaven
Worth far more than gold

Where there is love, there is hope
and where there is hope, come miracles
Congratulations on your new arrival
a true miracle of life

A girl, what a blessing
an angel from heaven
sent down in your care
to steal away your heart
forever

tip

Adapt the above verse for a
boy by changing the word
'girl' for 'boy'

A new baby boy
A bundle of joy
A real little lad
To drive you both mad
Celebrations are due
So we wish all of you
Our love and good wishes
With cuddles and kisses

Twenty fingers, twenty toes
Amazing how your family grows
Twice the fun, twice the care
Twice the love for us to share

To the proud Great Grandparents

What joy to be a mother
Or a father just the same
To see a little bundle
Who grows up
To take your name

But how joyous is the feeling
When this little child is grown
And bestows on you great treasures
Grandchildren of your own

Then another generation
From that lovely son you bore
Has a cause for celebration
A great-grand son you'll adore

tip

*This verse could be adapted
for grandparents by
changing some of the words
and omitting the last verse*

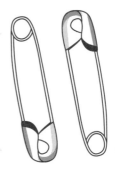

A baby arrived two by two
Surprised because we had no clue
One wears pink, the other blue
Celebrations are now due

A baby shower, how lovely
What good news you sent my way
I would love to join you all
Now that a baby's on the way
In celebrating such good fortune
And the miracle of creation
See you at the celebrations
It will be a grand occasion

A star fell down from heaven
And she landed in our arms
With all of Mummy's sweetness
And all of Daddy's charms

Double the love, double the joy
A baby girl and a baby boy

You'll be Mummy's little soldier
And Daddy's great big boy
You'll be Grandpa's little helper
You will bring us all such joy
I'm glad that I'm your Grandma
And I'm sending love to you
For a life that's full of laughter
In everything you do

Congratulations
on the birth of
your lovely twins
now you have twice
the fun and laughter
in your happy home
and twice the joy
in your hearts

Our little boy has just arrived
So tiny and precious too
We couldn't wait to share
This marvellous news with you

Our Son, a precious miracle
Has at last been sent our way
God has sent to us an Angel
Who brightens each new day

Our little miracle arrived at last
Captured our hearts and held on fast
He is the star up in our skies
And brings a sparkle to our eyes
A gift from God in every way
Celebrate, our son was born today

Curling hair, cute little nose
Beautiful eyes, wiggly toes
Tiny yawns, little sighs
Nursery rhymes, lullabies
Bonnets, bows, pretty lace
An angel's smile upon her face

We're all as happy as can be
Our new baby son has made us three

*O*ur precious
little boy
Is now sleeping in our arms
Weaving baby magic
As we fall for all his charms

Pink ribbons and bonnets
now lie on the chair
dresses and bootees
girl's clothes everywhere
she only arrived just hours ago
a girl in the family
and don't we just know

Our baby's arrived, so tiny and new
He didn't wait until he was due
All of a rush he decided to come
A lovely surprise for his Dad and Mum
So as we adjust to life full of mirth
Praise to the Lord for a miracle birth

The magical gift of adoption
has brought love into our home
as our precious little girl
joins our family at last

Our hearts are full of happiness
Our lives are full of love
Because we have our son at last
That we've been dreaming of

He is not flesh of my flesh
Nor is he bone of my bone
But by the love and will of God
They finally made him my own
My bond with him grew in my heart
With my love he has a brand new start

Our first child has arrived
She is so precious and small
We would like to share our joy
At her birth with one and all

Because she was so early
She can't come home quite yet
But eventually when you see her
You'll find a charm you won't forget

tip

*This verse is easily
adapted for a boy by
replacing he/she,
his/her, him/her*

Sorry

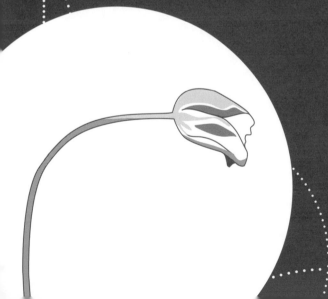

Sorry for everything not being as you hoped
maybe someday you will be able to accept
that it was just not meant to be

When it comes to eating humble pie
I'll forget I'm on a diet
I really am so sorry, my dear friend
Forgive someone old enough to know better

Sorry is such a little word
But it's sometimes hard to say
I hope it means a lot to you
Makes amends for yesterday

Your friendship means the world to me
What more can I do but pray
That you'll forgive me my stupidity
And we'll start again today

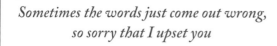

Sometimes the words just come out wrong,
so sorry that I upset you

*Such a small word, sorry
it can convey so many words
left unspoken, but still understood
between two close friends*

SORRY

*You are the most precious
person in my life
please accept my apology
I am so sorry*

*You were kind to invite me
so sorry I couldn't come
hope everything went to plan
and you had a lovely time*

There are so many words
but none so precious
as the word

SORRY

I'm sorry that you're feeling down
And things are rather blue
I hope this little message shows
How much I think of you

I'm sorry that you did not get
The news you needed badly
That the day was not the best yet
And it really ended sadly

But tomorrow brings new hope again
Another chance for you my friend
And think of all there is to gain
You will get there in the end

I heard the news was not great
No reason for you to celebrate
But then again just wait and see
Perhaps it was not meant to be
I'm sorry that you're feeling low
But life goes on I'm sure you know

Just to say........

sometimes life goes by so
quickly that I forget to
tell you that I love you
more each day

Christmas & New Year

Christmas is a time for sharing
may friends find a pathway to your home
bringing joy, love and happiness
at this special time of year

Raise glasses, give cheer
Bring in the New Year
It's a time to remember
Old friends and new

To reflect on the moments
Those that we hold dear
And to make resolutions
For the forthcoming year

Remember that at Christmas time
A little child was born
To bring us love, from God above
A gift we should adorn

So precious was His love for us
He gave His only son
So praise His name and share that love
With each and every one

May Christmas bring you happiness
To you and yours good cheer
But as you celebrate this time
Remember why it's here

*The reason for the season
is to give our thanks to God
for giving us the precious gift
of His only Son*

*May the miracle of Christmas
fill your hearts with
Joy and Love*

*Wishing you a very Merry Christmas
Full of love and joy and cheer
That lasts all over Christmas
And continues through next year*

May this wonderful season bring us
snowflakes falling like kisses from heaven
wrapping the earth in a blanket of love

May the New Year give you back
everything that you have given
may it return the love
you have bestowed on others
the kindness you have
shown along the way
and the fellowship you have earned
may it leave you looking forward
to another year with joy and contentment

*Promise me that you will
share a kiss with me
under the mistletoe
this Christmas
and forever more
my true love*

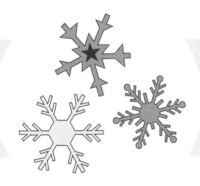

*Santa found your letter
And it filled his heart with joy
To receive a little note
From such a lovely little boy
He said you'd asked for kisses
For a Mum who you love so
And for extra special wishes
For a Christmas Day with snow
When it came to asking Santa
For some presents he did say
That he's granted all your wishes
Look for them on Christmas Day*

appy Holly
Days

*Love, Joy and Peace
from our house to yours*

*How quickly the time goes with each passing year
As we celebrate again with good Christmas cheer
May next year pass by slowly so that you can remember
Each month passing by from now to December
Take each day as it comes and make it all last
For all too soon they fade into the past
Life is so precious God gave us His love
Falling in snowflakes from heaven above*

*You're extra special people
Who always bring good cheer
So have a very Merry Christmas
And a peaceful Happy New Year*

*God sends us His love
In a blanket of snow
That makes our feet
And fingers glow*

With a partner like you
Today just stands apart
For festive love and wishes
Straight from my happy heart

You're a husband in a million
You make our marriage shine
Just glad I was so lucky
That you decided to be mine
May Christmas show you, darling
Amongst the festive love and glow
How much I care about you
And how I truly love you so

Son's First Christmas

Season's glad tidings
Love, peace and joy
To all of your family
And to your little boy
Who celebrates now
His first Christmas cheer
May you enjoy these moments
And the forthcoming year

Every Christmas time I find
I love you more and more
Thanks for being my companion
And the person I adore
God gave to me a present
More special than the rest
For when He gave me you, my love
He gave to me 'the best'

Thank You

You have a way of bringing joy
And laughter to each day
You brighten life for others
With the things you do and say
I would really like to thank you
For always being there
To lighten up the path of life
Because you really care

Just to say........

thank you for bringing
joy to each day

*Thank you
for caring about me
when you have your own
worries in life*

Thank you
for helping me up
when I stumbled and fell
on life's journey

Just to say........

thanks for being great
parents and always
being there when
I need you

Just wanted to tell you
how much your help and comfort meant to me
when I needed a friend
thank you for being there, for being you

Thank you for all your help
I could not have coped without you
you bring happiness into my house
and fill my world with laughter
making all things possible
no matter how hard life seems

Thank you
For all that you
Say and do
But most of all
For being you

Just to say........

thank you for coming
into my life and for
choosing to love me so

Thank you for listening to me
consoling me and inspiring me
when I felt vulnerable and alone
you restored my faith in life
and I am truly grateful

Thank you
for being there for me
when you should have been
somewhere else

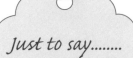

Just to say........

thank you
for coming to stay,
we really enjoyed
your company

I just pick up the telephone
And know you're on the end
There to listen to life's worries
Share my laughter, be my friend
Thank you for being so thoughtful
To you my loving thoughts I send

Just to say........

if I could choose my
parents I would have
chosen you both,
thanks for always
being there for me

Little deeds of kindness
Little words of love
You always make me happy
You are an angel from above

Thank You

Easter &
Religious

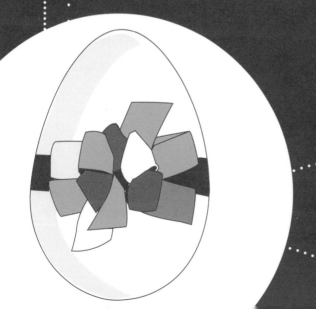

*May you feel the Lord's presence
not only at Easter, but always
for He revives the earth each springtime
and paints it in a rainbow of His love
to show us that the simple things in life
can bring us joy beyond compare*

*Praying that the Lord
fills your hearts with peace
holds you in His love
and blesses you with His grace
on this Holy Day and always*

*May the light of the Lord's love
shine upon you and your family
and brighten your daily lives
this Easter and always*

*So love, hope and faith
Should not die
God sent to us
A butterfly*

*Dragonflies and butterflies
fluttering through summer skies
beautiful and delicate
bringing hope and laughter
sent as a reminder of
God's creative hand*

*Wishing you an Easter time
filled with love, peace, happiness
and the joys of spring*

*May God keep you safe
in the palm of his hand
until we are together again*

*Put away your worldly goods this Easter
and remember that God gives us
all that we need to be truly happy
give thanks that He is risen*

*M*ay you and your family
enjoy the Festival of Baisakhi

May Wesak enlighten you as you celebrate Buddha's love for the human race

God colours our world in a rainbow of love

May these special Wesak celebrations surround you with Buddha's love and enlighten you with his wisdom

*May there be peace in your heart
and may the mercy and blessings of Allah
be upon you always*

Just to say........

*may God always walk
beside you as you
travel along the rugged
highway of life*

*The Fourth of July,
a time to celebrate our
heritage and great nation
a time to thank God
for all we were, all we are
and all we will be*

*Enjoy the Festival of Lights
and have a good Diwali*

*May
AHURA MAZDA
(The Wise Lord)
Bless you*

*Beyond darkness there is light
and wisdom lies beyond ignorance
May the Lord Buddha
guide you to the path of glory*

*During the fifteen days of your
New Year Celebrations
wishing you all that you wish for yourself*

*EID MUBARAK
Blessed Eid*

Seven days
Seven principles
Several ways for us
To make a change
In our family
Our community
Universally

Celebrate
Kwanzaa

*W*ishing you love, peace,
joy and happiness
to you and your loved ones at Chanukah

Here comes the May Queen
Amidst the flowers they sing
Morris Dancers follow her
Celebrating a new Spring

Wishing all of your family a joyful Diwali
full of love, peace and contentment

Christenings

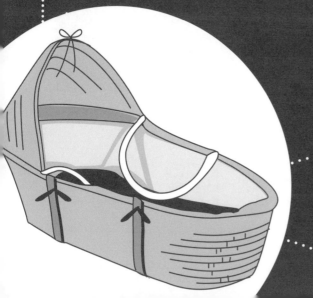

Those tiny toes that curl
And fingers closed so tight
A smile to warm your soul
And eyes that shine so bright
A true miracle of life
With soft and golden hair
Sent down from God above
A love for all to share
May God's love surround you all
On this special day as you give thanks
And praise His name

A child's smile is
one of life's
greatest blessings
a child's love is
a joy beyond compare
on this special day
give thanks to the Lord
for bestowing this treasure
into your safe keeping
for touching your life
with a miracle

*Blessings to you
and your bouncy
little Bundle of Joy
as you stand before the Lord
to give thanks for the miracle of life
that you now hold in your hands
may He love and protect you all forever*

*We bring you before God today
And bestow on you a name
For everyone to call you by
So you can seek your fame*

*We pray that you will find a way
To be good and kind and true
We hope that you will love God
And that He will love you too*

*Join us
to celebrate
our new arrival
as we thank God
for the miracle of life*

Before God we name you
In a house filled with love
As angels surround you
Blessings sent from above
To guard and protect you
In a world yet to see
As we nurture and guide you
To be all you can be

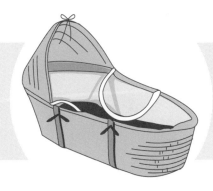

The angels are rejoicing
As they hear the news today
Another little angel
Has come to God so pray
That He will love them
Without question
If they live life as they should
Being kind to one another
Always choosing to be good

*May your child be blessed
with a loving and kind nature
as you bring him/her before God
in this baptism of faith
may his/her name be remembered
with fondness and admiration
in the years to come
and may he/she be
true to God always*

*May the love of God
protect your child always
and may He walk
with him/her forever
protecting body and soul*

*As you gather today
in the presence of God
may He bless your little one
with all of life's treasures*

As you all stand together
in Our Lord's House
may you feel His loving arms
wrapped around your family
as you call on Him to bless
you and your precious child
as you bestow a Christian name
so all may know and love him/her

tip

*Delete the last word
as appropriate*

In the name of the Lord
may the child you bring
before God today be blessed
with a life of goodness
and may all their dreams
become reality

Mother's Day

Mum, you are everything
I could ever hope to be
the mainstay of our family
always there for us
through good times and bad
and for that I truly love you

For all the times you worried
And for all the times you cared
For all the times we got upset
And for all the joys we shared
For each and every moment
And for every single day
For times you picked me up again
When I'd fallen on the way
I'd like to tell you Mother
Just how much it really means
To always have you there for me
Supporting all my dreams

HAPPY MOTHER'S DAY
To a wonderful Mother

When you become a Mother
It's a gift from God above
You depend on one another
Become bonded by a love
That is joy and pain together
Is as boundless as the sea
A love that lasts forever
And I know you will agree

WITH LOVE ON MOTHER'S DAY

Just to say........

I love you the most and
you are the best Mum
in the world

It seems like only yesterday
You wiped away my tears
Helped me grow and watched me play
What happened to those years
Now children I have of my own
Content and happy too
With grandchildren who love me
And it's all because of you
You really started something
When you fell in love with Dad
You are the perfect parents
And for that I'm really glad

Hope your Mother's Day is as wonderful as you

A
Mother
is the person
who sits at the head
of the family holding it so
firmly together in her own special
way binding it with love and devotion
as only she can for she gave us life nurtured
us and listened to our daily trials and tribulations
gave comfort and love when all was lost to us
she made us laugh when we wanted to cry
and picked us up when we were down
she asks nothing, expects nothing
and she deserves everything
God created Mothers
He created Love
in her for
us

For a lovely Daughter-in-Law

*Mother's Day, a perfect day
to tell you just how proud
we are that you love our Son
and Grandson so much
care for them, support them
and protect them as only you can
in your own special way*

*You are a lovely mummy
And I love you so
I'm sending you this card
Just so that you know*

HAPPY MUMMY'S DAY

Just to say........

*you are more than
a mother to me and
loved more than you
can imagine*

*I can't imagine days without
Your smile that made things right
Your calming voice I loved so much
When I woke up in the night
You nurtured me when I was young
Your love you never spared
I always knew that you were there
I always knew you cared
So on this special Mother's Day
I would truly like to say
You're a really lovely lady
So have an extra happy day*

It doesn't need a Special Day
To send love to you dear Mum
But thank you for the years
Gone by and all the years to come
For every time you've held my hand
And wiped the tears away
And sometimes for the words I said
But didn't mean to say
You're always there, a friend to me
My mentor all the way
So know I love you more than life
On this very special day

HAPPY MOTHER'S DAY

tip

*This verse can be for a
grandmother and great-
grandmother too, simply
substitute the word 'Mum'
for another*

*You fill my life with sunshine
And chase the clouds away
Make problems seem much smaller
With the loving things you say*

*I always know my welfare
Is in your heart and on your mind
No Mother could love me better
Be more thoughtful or more kind*

*So on this special day for Mothers
I want you to know that you
Are the person I would have chosen
To always see me through*

*I love you more than words can say
For each and everyday
You show how much you really care
And chase my blues away*

Happy Mother's Day

Just to say........

*you are the best Mum
in the world*

Father's Day

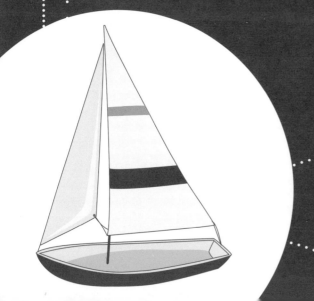

Special Wishes on Father's Day

You may not be my Father
But you're certainly my Dad
Someone I can rely on
When life seems really bad
To cheer me up and tell me
That I'm special and I know
You truly care and love me
And for that I love you so

tip

This verse right can be
for a grandfather and
great-grandfather too,
simply substitute the
word 'Dad' for another

Enjoy your day, Dad
it's our turn to run around
after you for a change
so enjoy the experience
and RELAX

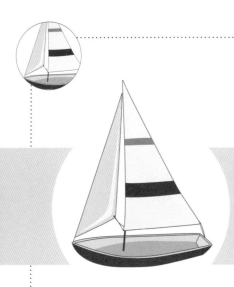

I hope one day
When I grow up
I turn out like you, Dad
Because you are
A Special Guy
And I'm pleased
That I'm your lad

You're not much good at D-I-Y
At golf you're even worse
When driving in a traffic jam
You sometimes start to curse
At cooking you are passable
At jokes you're really bad
But one thing you excel at
You're a really smashing Dad

Forgiving and trustworthy
Always there in a crisis
The first one to help anyone
Happy to stand in the background
Ever watchful over us
Responsible for our family

*No wonder there is a special day
for remembering the love and care
you give to everyone*

HAPPY FATHER'S DAY

Just to say........

*glad you stepped
into my life
For a Step-father you
are a great DAD*

You really are a special guy
Who fills my life with love
A father in a million
Sent down from God above
So enjoy this special day
With others of your kind
But know that every day you're special
And you're always on my mind

Just to say........

you're never
too old to need
your parents

Dad I could not imagine
A life without your smile
The little things you do for me
When you go that extra mile
And sometimes I forget to say
How much I love you so
Yet from laughter in your eyes
I think that you already know

HAVE A LOVELY FATHER'S DAY

Dad, no wonder I'm still single
And sitting on the shelf
How can I find the perfect man
When Mum kept him for herself
As a father you are great
In everything you do
I hope I find a guy one day
As reliable as you

Happy Father's Day

There may not be a bond of blood
that keeps us close at heart
but to me you are the perfect 'Dad'
you have been from the start
and as the years go by so fast
that they all blend into one
I will love you for the man you are
long after you have gone
forever in my memory
as the man who always cared
who always made the sun come out
on those magic days we shared

Dad, I really cannot tell you
Just how much you mean to me
No words could ever capture
A love as boundless as the sea
That wraps its arms around us
Makes a happy family
You make me very happy
And I'm really very glad
I can send my love this special day
To an extra special Dad

Just to say........

I love you more
every day

Good Luck
& New Job

A new job, how exciting
lots of training and new friends
so glad they saw your great potential
knew you'd get there in the end

Congratulations

Just to say........

travelling to new places
is an adventure you will
always treasure

Gone are those days of school books and toys
you have swapped them for working
with the men and the boys
in an office so high up
that you can't see the ground
but we know you'll be great there
the best thing around

Good Luck on your first day at work

*May Good Luck and Good Fortune
find you now and stay with you
throughout life's journey
and may happiness be your companion*

*We both feel so proud
of our little girl, the one we adore
good luck, in your new job
may good fortune open every door*

*May every day give you
new challenges and tasks
to make your new job
as interesting and rewarding
as you hoped it would be*

Best wishes on your retirement
Enjoy a rest that's overdue
Take pleasures in the finer things
That are awaiting you

Just to say........

as you move away from
home may you find all
you are searching
for in life

You are our ray of sunshine
Our winter flowers in the snow
We are glad you have this chance now
But we're sorry you must go
We wish you every joy in life
Success in all you do
Congratulations as you move away
And our best wishes too

We know you have it in you
To succeed at whatever you do in life
Believe in your dreams
And you will make them come true

We are sorry you're leaving today
For promotion and an increase in pay
We'll miss your sharp wit
But we know that you'll fit
In that job which is so far away

GOOD LUCK IN
YOUR NEW JOB

Congratulations are in order
You have done well today
We all knew that you could do it
More status and more pay

WELL DONE ON YOUR PROMOTION

*Well done on passing your training with flying colours
may the job be everything you hoped it would be
and may promotion be written in the stars for you
for you deserve the best of everything life has to offer*

We wish you every success
In your new job far away
It won't be the same without you
For you brightened up the day
You filled the place with kindness
Brought a smile upon each face
You will leave a void behind you
It will be hard to fill that space

Sending you a day full of sunshine
a heaven filled with rainbows
and a pocket full of dreams

GOOD LUCK FOR THE FUTURE

Glad to hear the news
That you passed the test
Knew you would get it
You always do your best
Enjoy all of your travels
Be them nearby or so far
Driving on life's highway
In your very own new car

*P*romotion,
how exciting
A new challenge and more pay
Our good wishes go out to you
On this very happy day

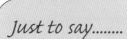

Just to say........

glad all your hard work
over the years gave you
the recognition
you deserve

You've set yourself a challenge
A new job to begin
With your lovely personality
We know you will fit in

CONGRATULATIONS

Get Well

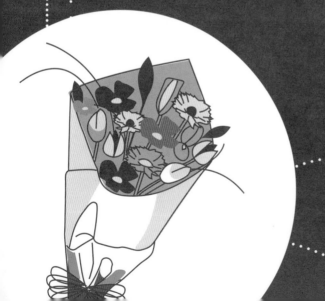

The doctors say you're poorly
And must stay in your bed
Until you feel much better
I'm sure that's what they said
Rest and recuperation
Will heal you in good time
So stay right there, relax, take care
Soon you'll be feeling fine

A bouquet of flowers I'm sending your way
As you're feeling poorly and blue
I hope that they cheer up your hospital stay
A reminder I'm thinking of you

So sorry you are poorly
And feeling rather low
Some rest and recuperation
Will do you good, you know
So listen to the doctors
And others that you meet
And soon you'll feel much better
And be back upon your feet

We're sorry that you're poorly
It must have been a scare
But listen to the doctors now
Rest, relax and now take care

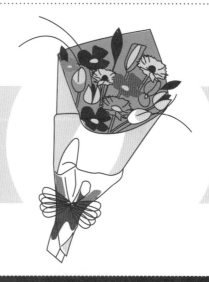

Just to say........

thank you for your
care and kindness

This note is full of sunshine
To brighten up the day
And bring with it a rainbow
To chase the blues away
May it make you feel much better
To know we think of you
So your spirits are uplifted
And recovery is soon due

With the miracle of life
Comes the miracle of recovery
Thanks to dedicated staff
And love of one another
Many thanks for all
You have done
To help me

May God take care of you
And angels nurse you back to health
For being fit and active
Is far more precious than any wealth
Forget the toil and trouble
Of a busy hectic life
For you are more important
To your family, kids and wife

Home is not the same without you
So just take care and soon
We will hear your lovely laughter
Filling all our rooms

The office is so quiet
No fun and laughter there
We all miss your
Light hearted banter
So rest now and take care
And soon you will be back
To brighten up the day
And make our lives
Much better in your
Very special way

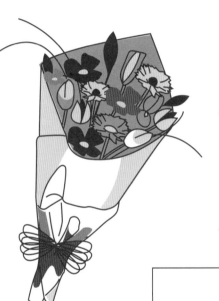

May God
Watch over you
Protect you
And love you
At this time
Until you
Recover

In each and every petal
Every leaf and stem you see
God's painted you a rainbow
Flowers of love from Him and me

I'm sending you these wishes
As you are not so well
Hope the rest does you good
And soon you'll be feeling swell

A healthy heart is a happy heart
Soon you will be on the mend
My dearest darling husband
My lover and my friend

Divorce & Sympathy

*Keeping you in our thoughts and prayers
at this difficult time*

*Know that in your special need
our love goes out to you
that you are constantly
in our thoughts and prayers
and God walks with you too*

*Know that you are in our thoughts
at this sad time
that you are in our prayers
in your time of need
and that your wellbeing
is close to our hearts always*

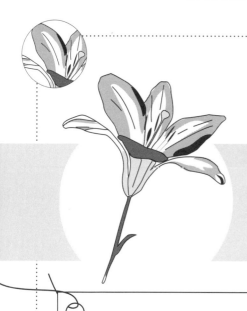

*D*uring this
difficult time
may you feel
God's loving arms
around you
and His love
in your heart

Gather strength from those around you
Though you feel like letting go
Let God's loving arms surround you
Because He loves you so
Know that others feel like you do
Feel the sadness and the pain
So open up your heart to Him
Don't ever feel alone again

Just to say........

may sadness turn to
happy memories
with the passing
of time

In your life together
there were thousands of kisses
none as special as the first
and none so sad as the last
sadly departed from this earth
in your loss, may your love re-capture
memories long forgotten,
gestures and words of comfort
and may God keep you in His love
until you are re-united
in the House of the Lord

Just to say........

*you're all in my
heart, always*

There is nothing in life than cannot be overcome
You may not be a wife but you're still a loving Mum
As time goes by you will realise there is more to life than men
And when that day comes round, then you will learn to live again
In the meanwhile, be sure that I am always here for you
To pick you up each time you fall, a faithful friend who's always true

Look at this milestone in your life
as a new beginning
rather than the end of an era
turn heartache into laughter
by seeking out new adventures
always be true to yourself
and take time to praise yourself
for all you have achieved
to be where you are today

Just to say........

thank you
for always
being there

At the end of the tunnel, there is always light
The brightest day always follows the darkest night
For every ebb, there is a flow
So let the sadness and hurt you feel just go

Let the light and brightness flow into your life
You are your own person now, not just an ex-wife
Give no heed to what belongs firmly in the past
As you take your place centre stage at last

Just to say........

your comforting words
were just what
I needed

Invitations

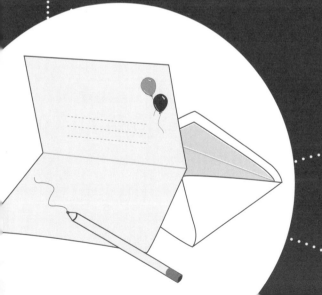

Twelve months of growing
And learning to have fun
So I can have a party
Because today
I'm ONE

Times sure flies when everything is fun
Please come to my party
I'm going to be
ONE

Come to my party for a day filled with fun
We'll eat ice cream and cake when it's all done

Blow up balloons
Celebrations are due
Have fun at my party
Because I will be TWO

Hair tied in ribbons
My dress is all new
The party's at my house
Because I am TWO

A party is planned
with magic and fun
Celebrations are due,
they are second to none

A love so beautiful and so true
A life together beginning anew
A bond so strong, a link, a tie
A love that they cannot deny

Come and celebrate, the union of
two people who are so in love

As you have shared in their lives
by your friendship and love
the honour of your presence is requested
at the marriage of:

_____

Just to say........

thank you
for your lovely gift

A fancy dress party, well what will you wear?
As long as you come we don't really care
Witches or warlocks, lady or lord
We can guarantee that you'll never be bored
Magical spells are booked for the night
With spooky old stories to give you a fright
So dress up to scare us, come on, don't be mean
So we can all be together on this Halloween

Beautiful Beginnings lead to Happily Ever Afters
so please join us in a celebration of love
a commitment between two people who
were truly meant to be together

We really are excited to share our news with you
The man I love has asked me and I replied 'I Do'
We have not thought of venues nor have we set a date
All that comes in due course but for now come celebrate
The ring is simply wonderful I can't believe it's true
I want to tell the whole world so I'm starting off with you
Pass around the good news so the party goes real well
Celebrations are in order so invite everyone you tell

All of these years, a single life
She's soon to be the perfect wife
Her heart is taken, love's found a way
So let's party on down before the big day

Just to say........

*I had a wonderful
time, let's do it
again soon*

The man of her dreams has swept her away
And soon it will be their wedding day
So I have a suggestion, girls if I may
One last weekend full of play

The date is fast approaching
So now's the perfect time
To get all the girls together
Before the wedding bells do chime

Miscellaneous

*Let love
and happiness
surround you
in a garden
full of flowers*

*May all your dreams
Come true
And may life be good
To you*

*Live life
as if
every day
is the
last one
and you
will have
no regrets*

*May your day
be happy
and filled
with love
and joy*

*May you find the faith
you need tomorrow
in the love
you experience today*

*You are a star in every way
and no-one shines so bright*

Sending you stardust
to sparkle your life
and fill your days
with smiles and laughter

Just to say........

goodbye for now, until
we meet again

A smile in the right place
Can chase away sadness
A smile at the right time
Can make life seem fine

*Wishing you
gentle showers of
sunshine and flowers
and rainbows
to colour your day*

*Spring
brings
new life
green shoots
buds
and blossoms*

*Summer
brings
warm sunshine
ice creams
sandcastles
and seashells*

*Autumn
brings
glorious colours
squirrels gathering
harvest fruits
and flowers*

Just to say........

enjoy your holiday
rest, relax and leave
the pets to me

*Winter
brings
magical snowflakes
frosty mornings
cosy homes
and Christmas*

I'm so impressed by all of your hard work well done you!

Take time to smell the flowers in God's lovely garden

*L*earn from yesterday
Live for today
Dream for tomorrow

*S*orry your cat
is poorly
hope he/she will soon be
in Purrfect condition

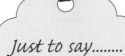

Just to say........

*thank you for pet and
house sitting – you
were marvellous*

*Congratulations
I believe you have
the patter of tiny paws,
may all your troubles
be little ones*

187

Suppliers

UK WHOLESALERS

Crafts Too Ltd
Unit 2 Kingstons Ind Estate
Eastern Road
Aldershot
Hants GU12 4YA
Tel: (+44) (0)1252 330024
www.crafts-too.com
*Wholesaler of craft products
importing and distributing ranges
from USA & Europe*

Design Objectives
www.docrafts.co.uk
*Contact them directly through the
website or contact Magna Craft on
01730 815555*

Kars Creative Wholesale
www.kars.biz
*Visit website for your nearest UK
stockists of their craft products.
Based in Holland and the UK
see further listings for Europe*

Personal Impressions
Curzon Road
Chiltern Industrial Estate
Sudbury
Suffolk CO10 2XW
www.richstamp.co.uk
Tel: (+44) (0)1787 375241
*Visit website or call for your nearest
stockists of their craft products from
USA & UK importers of products
listed in USA section*

Pergamano UK
Curzon Road
Chiltern Industrial Estate
Sudbury
Suffolk CO10 2XW
www.richstamp.co.uk
Tel: (+44) (0)1787 375241
*Sole UK importer of Pergamano
parchment craft products
Contact for your nearest
Pergamano tutor and retailer*

UK RETAILERS

Arty and Crafty Supplies
Genestic Cottage
Monkton
Honiton
Devon EX14 9QH
Tel: (+44) (0)1404 45883
Email: judith@artyandcrafty.
demon.co.uk
www.buycraftsonline.co.uk
*Online art and craft retailer
specialising in card making – sorry
no personal callers. Retailers of
products from Personal Impressions
and Pergamano UK*

*Arty and Crafty Supplies for card
making, rubber stamping, parchment
craft and art projects. We supply
goods from Personal Impressions,
Pergamano, Funstamps, Inca
Stamps, Fiskars, Marvey, Tsukineko,
Artistic Wire and American
Traditional Stencils with new brand
names updated regularly. If you are a
crafter or artist visit our website,
www.buycraftsonline.co.uk*

Craft Creations
Ingersoll House
Delamere Road
Cheshunt
Hertfordshire EN8 9HD
Tel: (+44) (0)1992 781900
www.craftcreations.co.uk
Greeting card blanks and general craft retailer. Mail order or contact for stockists

Fred Aldous Ltd
37 Lever Street
Manchester M1 1LW
Tel: (+44) (0)1613 262477
www.fredaldous.co.uk
Established in 1886, this is an Aladdin's Cave of art and craft materials. Craft workshops also available

Hobbycraft Stores
Tel: 0800 027 2387
www.hobbycraft.co.uk
General craft retailer. Mail order available or call for your nearest store

The ranges of craft products listed here are imported into the UK by Personal Impressions – see the UK listing for address

American Traditional Designs
442 First NH Turnpike
Northwood
NH 03261
Tel: 1 800 448 6656
www.americantraditional.com
Embossing stencil manufacturers. Visit website for products and local stockist

Artistic Wire Limited
752 North Larch Avenue
Elmhurst
IL 60126
Tel: 630 530 7567
www.artisticwire.com
View a full range of wires and accessories and local stockist

Art Institute Glitter
712 N Balboa Street
Cottonwood
Arizona 86326
Tel: toll free [877] 909-0805
www.artglitter.com
Projects, products and a gallery online with details of suppliers in your area

Carl Products
1876 South Elmhust Road
MT. Prospect
IL 60056
Tel: 1 847 956 0730
www.carl-products.com
Craft products for cutting paper

Fiskars Brands, Inc.
School, Office & Craft
2537 Daniels St Madison,
WI 53718
Tel: 1 866 348 5661
www.fiskars.com
Craft products for punching, cutting and decorating paper

Suppliers

Magic Mesh
PO Box 8
Lake City
MN55041
Tel: 651 345 6374
www.magicmesh.com
Full range of products, project ideas for card making and scrapbooking with stockist list

Pritt Products
Tel: 0800 321 0253
www.prittproducts.com
Pritt is the worldwide expert in paper gluing, correction, and has products for all crafting needs

Ranger Industries Inc
15 Park Road
Tinton Falls
NJ 07724
Tel: 732 389 3535
www.rangerink.com
Visit website to see vast range. Suppliers of products for rubber stamping

Tsukineko, Inc
17640 NE 65th Street
Redmond, WA 98052 USA
Tel: (425) 883 7733
www.tsukineko.com
Manufacturers of unique ink products and craft accessories that fire your imagination

Uchida Of AmericaCorp
3535 Del Amo Boulevard
Torrance
CA 90503
Tel: 1 800 541 5877
www.uchida.com
Manufacturers of art and craft materials for card making, scrapbooking and art projects

USArtQuest Inc
7800 Ann Arbor Road
Grass Lake
MI 49240
Tel: 517 522 6225
www.usartquest.com
Visit the website for tips and techniques

Kars Creative Wholesale
Industriweg 27
Industrieterrein 'De Heuning'
Postbus 97
4050 EB Ochten
The Netherlands
Tel: (+31) (0) 344 642864
www.kars.nl
Visit website or call for your nearest stockists of general craft products

JEJE Produkt V.O.F.
Verlengde Zuiderloswal 12
1216 BX Hilversum
The Netherlands
Tel: 035 624 6732
www.jejeprodukt.nl
Suppliers of Sandy Art product range, stickers and adhesives

Pergamano International
Postbus 86
1420 AB Uithoorn
The Netherlands
Tel: (+31) (0) 297 526256
www.pergamano.com
Parchment craft manufacturers.

AUSTRALIA

ParchCraft Australia
PO Box 1026
Elizabeth Vale
South Australia 5112
www.parchcraftaustralia.com
*Visit website to find your local
stockists of these metal parchment
craft tools*

CANADA

Magenta Rubber Stamps
2275 Bombbardier Street
Sainte-Julie
Quebec J3H 3B4
Tel: 450 922 5253
www.magentastyle.com
*Visit the website for full
product details and to locate
your local stockist*

SOUTH AFRICA

Brasch Hobby
10 Loveday Street South
Selby
Johannesburg
South Africa 2001
Tel: +27 11 493 9100
www.brasch.co.za
*Manufacturers and distributors of
Genuine Heritage Craft Products*

About the Author

Born and bred in Cheshire she moved to Manchester when
she married Colin. After raising their children James and
Deborah she opened an Arts & Crafts Centre specialising in
handmade cards where her love of creative writing lead to these
verses especially for card makers. Although she will always be a
Northern Lass, Judith Wibberley now resides in the beautiful
Otter Valley in Monkton, Devon with her husband, where she
writes and runs a craft website, **www.buycraftsonline.co.uk.**

Index